MY WAY

Perspectives of a Riot

MY WAY

Perspectives of a Riot

John Werchon

Published in Australia by Sid Harta Books & Print Pty Ltd,
ABN: 34632585293
23 Stirling Crescent, Glen Waverley, Victoria 3150 Australia
Telephone: +61 3 9560 9920
E-mail: author@sidharta.com.au

First published in Australia 2022
This edition published 2022

Cover design, typesetting: WorkingType (www.workingtype.com.au)

John Werchon
My Way: Perspectives of a Riot
ISBN: 978-1-925707-77-9
pp96

ABOUT THE AUTHOR

As I begin this journey and try to recall my past for good or bad, I am sitting in a *Donga* at a camp site at the top of Australia in a place called Gove (Nhulunbuy) in the Northern Territory. We are supposed to be in a tropical paradise, but the reality is far from this. The beauty of the country is undeniable but is marred by a myriad of human issues. The earth itself is only held fast by those who are strong enough to control it, giving rise to the notion that there is always another who wants what you have.

When you think about the values of life, for me, it really only comes down to being a Christian; having a loving family; being supportive of friends; maintaining good health and understanding where the next person is coming from. The people closest to you and their wellbeing is of the utmost importance — life is short, and you only get one go at it, so adjust your mistakes as you travel and help others along the way, for at the end of the road, only God will judge our journeys.

John E. Werchon.

John Werchon and (L to R) Angel, Nasku & Kimba

John Edward Werchon, 1990. Correctional Officer, Yatala Labour Prison Adelaide, South Australia

CITATION

On 6 May, 1996, a number of prisoners seized control of B-Division, Yatala Labour Prison.

The actions of these prisoners placed in jeopardy the safety and well being of several Department for Correctional Services officers serving at Yatala Labour Prison at the time of the incident.

In containing and finally resolving the incident, departmental officers were assisted by their colleagues in the South Australian Police, in particular the STAR Force, the South Australian Ambulance Service and the Metropolitan Fire Service.

During the 11 hours over which the incident took place, the prisoners caused serious injury, stress and trauma to four prison officers serving in B-Division, until their release could be effected.

John Edward Werchon,

throughout this serious incident the actions of these prisoners put your personal safety and well-being at grave risk, causing you, your family, friends and departmental colleagues considerable fear and anxiety.
Despite these harrowing circumstances, you demonstrated courage, fortitude and calmness which assisted the negotiators in their difficult task of resolving the incident without the loss of life.

Accordingly, I, John Paget, Chief Executive, award John Edward Werchon the Exemplary Conduct Medal.

I hereby formally commend your actions which were in accordance with the highest traditions established by officers of the Department, who have loyally served the people of South Australia since the Department was formed.
I also extend my gratitude and best wishes to your family and colleagues who have endured and supported you, both during and after this incident.

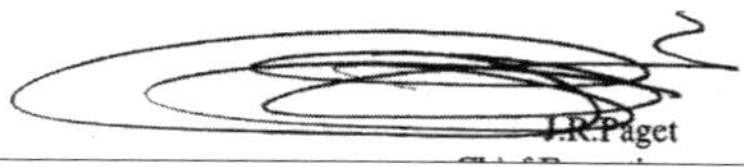

J.R.Paget

*John Werchon, Commissionaire, 1979,
Regine's Nightclub, Light Square, Adelaide,
South Australia*

John Werchon — 1974. Hotel porter, Amsterdam, Netherlands.

DEDICATION/ ACKNOWLEDGEMENTS

Dedicated to my loving family.

Albeit long after the event, I wish to extend my personal thanks to my fellow Correctional Officers and the responding Police Officers, whose bravery I can attest to.

AUTHOR NOTE, DISCLAIMER

In describing people involved, their actions, and events as they unfolded, I've chosen to change names for privacy purposes, and as a means of differentiating for clarity; however, note to the curious reader that the Yatala riot and hostage situation is a matter of public record.

Preface

... When one reads the post-riot Department Review, there is an endless list of recommendations for the future running of the prison, and unsurprisingly, the re-introduction of well-established control procedures that were strongly in place in 1989, talk about DeJa'Vu. It would seem hindsight really is a beautiful thing ...

John E. Werchon

I was a man in the middle of a situation, just like the other 'players' in the riot, all of us had roles to fulfil, some ill-fitting. Often, it's the little things that are evoked the most readily, and when in dire trouble, I recalled my father's advice — 'Try not to go to ground.' When an event leaves teeth marks, often it's your perceptions, common sense and memories that can surprise and sustain.

The following words provide my personal account of the prison environment in place early in my career and the events leading to and after a hostage situation and riot.

Contents

Chapter 1

SWORN-IN CADETS

I graduated as a Correctional Officer on the third of March 1989 after a training course that commenced on the nineteenth of January — an introductory 12-week course, number 86, which was modelled on Semi Military Training Principles. Twenty-six cadets were fitted out *en mass* in uniforms; propelled through regulation marching drills; taught Self-Defence, Fitness Training, Firearm Training; and were instructed in the academic and legislative

January 1989 Correctional Officer John Werchon — Standing Left-Most, Back Row.

environment commensurate with our future role as Correctional Officers.

During basic training, and later in the workforce, we cadets were also taught that the safety of other officers was mandatory, as was the duty of care owed to both fellow officer and prisoner; these being essential requirements of Correctional Officers. Rudimentary training on the dangers associated with this line of work becomes invaluable in the prison world, such as the way the door of a cell will open and where you should be positioned when it does, and procedures for walking around corners. Dealing with trip wires in the workshops; objects placed in food; razor blades in shirt lapels or under a bed frame, mattress or chair seat; shoelaces and belts for strangulation; prisoner hygiene and diseases they may carry; spit; biting; pencils — all tantamount to the fact that *any* object is a weapon, and one must be aware of this and learn to respond appropriately.

As a team, we marched into our role as sworn-in Correctional Officers on the third day of March 1989. I was assigned for commission at the Yatala Labour Prison and when I walked through those gates for the first time, the reality of what I was stepping into struck me like a lead brick as this was 'Towering Walls'. Razor wire sat on top of walls and fences, complete with out-perimeter barbed-wire fences, which had electrified sensor zones and heavy gates. A cold stark environment, this was a world of its own, and one where the *real* training was about to begin.

In those days, cadets were on probation for one year, during which time we were constantly trained in and monitored for our suitability as Correctional Officers. I suppose in a way, probation provided a mutual 'out' for the cadet and Correctional Department, as officer breakdown was quite common, due to it being a difficult environment in which to work.

In 1989 the prisoner control was very strict and the then Manager of the prison — who was from the old school — used to walk proudly and freely throughout the prison with his Swagger Stick (a ceremonial wooden baton — an old British officer tradition) under his armpit, hat on his head, wearing a crisp, pressed uniform that reminded me of the role played by Alec Guinness in the movie *Bridge on the River Kwai*.

Prisoners would present themselves for parade and inspection in the yard when going to the workshops. The process was extremely regimented and regulated, but interestingly the prisoners seemed to like this style of discipline as they knew where they stood, now being creatures of schedule and regulation. But with the changing of the Guard, a new CEO complete with departmental procedural instructions for day-to-day dealing with prisoners; a new thought pattern was being presented to the officer. The new stances were purported to make the prisoner a better person upon release, thus slowly morphing officer's roles from Duty of Care to that of carer or case manager, and counsellor.

Effectively, endeavouring to understand the underlying reasons for prisoner's crimes and behavioural patterns, and listening to their grievances, provided a mechanism enabling more empowered prisoners and subsequent self-ownership of their correctional experience. Thus, rules were slowly relaxed, encouraging the CEO of the day to want officers to 'connect more' with the prisoner. The old adage — 'You Do the Crime; You Serve the Time' was rapidly changing.

With empowerment, the aftereffects produced fewer officers and less control, which equated to a greater security risk to both officer and establishment. Replacing the more-seasoned officer with an academically qualified (yet ill-prepared) rookie, and the offering of once-in-a-lifetime redundancy packages reduced staff to dangerously low levels, as viewed by most within the ranks.

Prisoner committees and prisoner liaison spokespeople — who now had significantly more freedom of inter-unit movement — comprised the perceived 'new order'. With written and logged records of prisoner movement also overly relaxed, prisoners were now able to move between designated areas in greater numbers, while officer morale under the watch of the current CEO slowly eroded, creating apathy within the prison.

> As an interesting aside — when one reads the post-riot Department Review, there is an endless list of recommendations for the future running of the prison, and unsurprisingly, the *re*-introduction of well-established control procedures that were strongly in place in 1989, talk about *deja'vu*. It would seem hindsight really is a beautiful thing ...

In my learning phase I had the good fortune to be guided by an officer who had been in the job for some twenty years; he was Welsh and had a great singing voice, which at times he would use to calm agitated prisoners down. Among many things, he also taught me *not* to make a commitment to a prisoner you could not keep; to give precise, direct orders and learn the meaning of the word 'no'. Respect was the key, he advocated, saying that they had put themselves in prison and your role was not to punish but provide a Duty of Care for their wellbeing. As part of my duties as a Correctional Officer I'd restrained prisoners using the approved required force, which naturally was fuel for discontent for some inmates, but up until the riot I had never been assaulted or threatened.

The only exception to this was an attack some time prior to the riot upon the house my family and I lived in, and an assault upon myself where I was hit on the head by a beer bottle that caused a minor laceration. As a Correctional Officer, it's a given that you should only wear your uniform while on duty and avoid letting too many people know of your occupation, as prisoners will eventually be released. This incident occurred because my neighbour — who was being harassed by a group of young men living in the same street — out of concern for himself and his family, had mentioned to them that I was a law enforcement officer. On the night of the incident the neighbour had come to our house asking for assistance in speaking to them. The police were called, and I went over to talk to them with my wife Liisa, though the neighbour had disappeared by this time, leaving us vulnerable and exposed. Liisa and I reached several men sitting on the fence, and after asking them to stop throwing objects at the house, I turned my back on them and at the same time was hit on the head with a beer bottle. By the time I recovered from the shock of this, the police were arriving to take control.

During the ensuing court proceedings, it was revealed that most of the youths had served time. After the court case and with some gentle persuasion from both the community in general and the youth's landlord, who had explained their perspectives to the court, the youths were evicted from the house and normal life resumed.

On adopting a Correctional Officer's role, one's whole world is exposed to the criminal element in society. To highlight an example: only weeks after commencing work as a Correctional Officer, a prisoner approached me one morning asking how my family was. During the conversation and to my surprise, the prisoner let it be known to me that he had knowledge of the school my girls attended. This was not a threat, rather it was to convey to me that they had the means and the wherewithal to acquire the general knowledge necessary to then access my entire life. As my house was within four kilometres of the prison, this was a sobering realisation ...

I commenced work at Yatala Labour Prison not knowing that it would be my last day of work at the prison as a Correctional Officer, and the start of a new commitment in my life and a stronger bond with my wife and three girls.

The day began with the sun shining and a light crisp feeling in the air. I had been for a run early in the morning with our dogs — German Shepherd Zulu, and Toy Poodle Coco.

At approximately 15:05 hours a nightmare began that would last until 02:23 hours the following morning. Along with three other officers, I was taken hostage by the prisoners of B1 Top West (32 prisoners). Warwick Jones was released at 15:39 and Neil Smyth at 21:34. Daniel Smith and I were held until the final countdown at approximately 02:23, Tuesday morning.

Chapter 2

DUTIES, ROUTINES AND EXPERIENCES

Unlock

Daily duties on day shift entailed either a 07:30 start or 08:00 briefing by the senior officer of the day. Each unit would have one or two trustee prisoners who would be allowed out after the master key unlock to prepare the food server, clean the officers' station and do a little mopping and general cleaning.

After the daily officer briefing, we would then open the cell doors so that the prisoners could shower and have breakfast before the start of their daily routines. Some prisoners would go to the recreation yard, others to education, medical appointments, escorts, and to the workshops. Officers worked on a well-organised time schedule without delays.

In my first few years at the Yatala Labour Prison the schedule was extremely tight and thus provided better protection for the officer — most units housed up to thirty-two prisoners with two rostered duty officers. In the mornings, the senior officer of the day shift would unlock each cell with the prison master key and then two officers, with another officer standing by the entrance barrier of the wing, would proceed to the far end of the unit and systematically inspect each cell separately while the prisoner stood by the door with his dirty laundry and any rubbish in his hand. An inspection was made of the cell; if it was not up to requirements, we would secure the prisoner in his cell and continue to the next cell, returning later to check on their cell, and if the cell then was to standard, the prisoner would then proceed down to the Wing Barrier. After laundry and rubbish disposal, the prisoner then returned to their cell to be locked securely within and we would then move on. After all of the cells on either side had been routinely inspected, a group of four officers would enter and move from unit to unit, assisting with final opening of the cell doors. Two officers would walk to the far end of the wing and open the cell doors as they moved towards the Wing Barrier entrance, which was then secured, the prisoners now free to move around the wing.

When it was time to serve breakfast, only two prisoners at a time were allowed into the general area between the wings where there was a food-servery section, and they returned to their respective wings before the next two prisoners were allowed out. Escorts always consisted of two or more officers, depending on how many prisoners were in transit, and if they were high risk, they would be handcuffed.

At lunch time the inmates in the recreation yards would return to their units; others would have lunch in their respective areas — education room, infirmary, holding cells or workshops, after which they could stay in their wings to make phone calls or just relax; others would go back to the recreation yard. There was always a careful and constant record kept of prisoner movement.

Lock-Up

Between the hours of 15:00 and 15:20 the prisoners would again return to their units from the recreation yards, workshops, education rooms, and infirmary. They were allowed to move in groups of eight prisoners at a time (which facilitated greater control) to their respective units. In B Division, which had three levels, the return movement would start with the bottom floor. When the first group of prisoners arrived, they would be secured in their respective wings and then the next group would follow, until all of the prisoners had returned to the unit. The same routine would be repeated on the second and top floors; when the prisoners arrived in their unit they would shower and get ready for mealtime then lock-up. Once all the prisoners had returned to their units the evening meal routine would start — only two prisoners at a time would be allowed into the servery section, the only exception being the trustees who served the meals.

After all the meals had been served, it would be close to 16:00 hours and the final lock-up routine for the day would commence. A group of four officers would again come into the unit to assist with the lock-down; the only difference being that this time we would start at cells nearest the Wing Barrier entrance and work our way to the end of the unit. After that the senior officer for night duties would come through and double lock each cell with the master key. The master key was always kept in the control room of the prison away from the units, which meant that night duty officers did not have access to the cells.

In the final step of the procedure, two officers would go from cell to cell to collect the cutlery and plates and then pour tea or coffee for those prisoners wanting a cup, as they were completely locked down (this was done through the cell trapdoor). Time to now sign off for the day and hand over to the night duty officers, who generally numbered two for each division.

Change of Guard

By 1996 this tight control schedule had well and truly passed with the changing of the guard. A Swing Shift had also been introduced to allow for the prisoners to have more time out of their cells, which was my scheduled rostered shift on the day of the riot.

Swing Shift was 11.30 am 'til 7.30 pm, so instead of the usual lock-down at 16:00, the lock-down would start around 19:00. In light of the self-ownership policy, and the CEO's desire for officers to connect more with prisoners, instead of officers manning the recreation yard entrance gate, prisoner movement was monitored from a revolving gate in a secured room overlooking the area and electronically controlled by one officer some distance away.

Escort-to-prisoner ratio could be as much as eight prisoners to one officer and the handcuffing of hard-line prisoners was now a thing of the past — a result of the overall 'relaxation' process. On leaving the prison though, all prisoners were still handcuffed as a precautionary measure. Opening the unit wing cells now involved just two officers going into the wing and systematically opening the cell doors without any inspection being conducted, and four, sometimes six, prisoners were allowed into the food-servery section at one time. Lock-up for the night was reduced to just two officers going into the wing and securing the cells, with the master key lock-down process still in place.

Each division was permitted a prisoner committee and select prisoners acting in a liaison role were allowed to move from floor to floor to talk with other, more troubled, prisoners.

> Later as it happened, two prisoners — who were the ring leaders of the riot — were able to slip through the system and gain entry to the top floor and thus take myself and fellow officers by surprise.

Unbeknown to me, as I had been away from the prison for some days, after having arrived for my shift, I had my duty position changed with no explanation. I was to later find out that the prison administration was aware of dissent within B division and with rumours circulating to the effect that certain officers were under threat. The management decision was to change rostered duties on the day, which is how I ended up as a Unit Officer in B Top on the day of the riot. (The *Freedom of Information* document, that incidentally took over two years to come to light, confirms this sequence of events.)

Added to the mix, prison management in their wisdom placed middle-floor-level Protectees in B Division — persons charged with offences such as child molesting (paedophiles); elder abuse; sex offenders and other inmates who required protection from the mainstream prisoners, for example those owing drug debts to fellow prisoners. These prisoners often feared for their safety, particularly in the exposed environment of the mainstream prison. Referred to as 'Protectees', they were afforded protection from other prisoners within the system as they were considered 'free targets' for assault and abuse by other inmates. A Protectee was 'Marked for Life' and rarely accepted into the mainstream prison.

Another potential contributing factor to the ensuing riot within the hierarchy, was that top-floor-level mainstream high-security prisoners serving long-term sentences. They had committed some of the most violent of crimes including murder and co-existed with bottom-floor-level prisoners who were considered non-conformists within the prison system — a veritable 'recipe for disaster'. Stuck in the middle were Protectees, who had to be moved during the riot due to the fear that if the top floor prisoners broke out, they would proceed to the middle floor to do them harm.

Experiences

Prisoners get time off for good behaviour and unfortunately also achieve time off due to prison overcrowding, which was an issue that Yatala Labour Prison experienced at the time. Yatala was a high-security prison and a prisoner had to serve approximately one third of his time there before being eligible for transfer to a lower-security prison.

Prior to embarking on an escort, written orders to follow were given (along with the mandatory sign off) and staff were advised of the specific route the journey would be taking, which, for added security, also differed from the route back. Prior to leaving the prison holding cells, the prisoners were strip searched and changed into their civilian clothes, handcuffed and in some cases, further handcuffed to a Correctional Officer; however, on the occasion as described below, this was not a requirement.

A seemingly routine escort duty to the Supreme Court in the City of Adelaide resulted in a prisoner making a bid for freedom. For transport we used ambulance-style vehicles, which were fitted out with individual cells, approximately eight to ten cells per vehicle. Used for most escorts, if we were escorting a highly dangerous prisoner, a police backup escort was provided. On this particular occasion, I was with a female officer transporting six prisoners, one of whom was serving a sentence of over fifteen years; yet none of the prisoners were deemed high risk and were merely attending routine court hearings to review their sentencing time or court cases for other crimes committed.

With the prisoners loaded and secured in their individual cells, we proceeded to the South Australian Supreme Court located opposite Victoria Square next to the Adelaide market. Procedurally, on leaving Yatala Labour Prison, the officers obtained permission to leave via radio, avoiding in-transit radio use for security purposes. On arrival at the Supreme Court, the officers once again radioed the Supreme Court control room, so that court staff could open the Sally Port Doors — the entrance to a secure garage area. Upon entering the garaged area, the Sally Port Doors were locked securely behind the vehicle and officers began the prisoner unloading process. Prisoners remained handcuffed until they were locked in the court cells. The handover process began with a path down to the underground cells via an entrance door, then into a lift, which would take the prisoners to be secured in cells and into the hands of the court officers. Delivering officers would then wait in a mess room until it was time for the return journey to Yatala. All Supreme Court entrances had intercoms and were monitored by camera and for additional security measures, control of the doors — including the Sally Port Doors — rested with the court control room.

Prisoners can be opportunists and on this occasion prior to the return journey the opportunity arose for one of the prisoners. After again handcuffing the six prisoners in a reverse of the arrival procedure, we moved to the lift then up to ground level. All was proceeding as normal — the female officer was in the lead, followed by the six prisoners, with the prisoner serving the 15-year sentence behind her, with myself at the rear. The leading officer pushed the intercom button requesting the door to be opened, and as it did, the front prisoner hit her on the back of the head, knocking her to the ground and he then ran.

In the short time it took me to get to where she was laying, the prisoner was just exiting the Sally Port Doors, which were wide open. Fortunately, she was okay, and also fortunately the remaining prisoners did not attempt to flee, perhaps recognising the futility of such an action. I contacted the control room via intercom and briefly appraised them of the situation, then I pushed the prisoners back inside and closed the door, pursuing the escapee, who by then had a good hundred-metre lead.

This proved to be a merry chase through the streets of Adelaide, as I could not see him and relied on hurried directions given by the public who saw this handcuffed male running and knocking people over. I did not succeed in catching him, but a few hours later he was found by police hiding down by the railway line near West Terrace. He did tell me later, though, that I was close and as he had run out of puff, he simply stepped into a shop doorway moments before I ran past him.

This sort of incident generally happened on the fly and is more the result of an opportunity grasped, which you can't always be entirely ready for. On reflection, somehow the Supreme Court control room operators had made a mistake.

With some inmates it is a 'revolving door' scenario, whereby I have walked a prisoner down Peter Brown Drive to Grand Junction Road — a duty requirement in those days — said the usual: 'I trust that we don't see you again, Bloggs.' [name changed for privacy] A casual stroll back; stop-off at the Main Gate for a chat; back to my rostered position in the holding cells, which is where all prisoners who enter–exit the prison are processed, only to be handed the duty of checking Bloggs in again. The police had been waiting for him just down the Grand Junction Road to arrest him for another crime he had committed ...

Being a Correctional Officer is not always a pleasant occupation and prisoners can become institutionalised, particularly when they have served many years in prison. Incarceration can become a way of life — they have security, clothing, food, recreation and some become totally dependent on the system, the dependency creating situations that many may find hard to understand. While on duty I have seen the end result of prison life for some inmates. Among the ranks, prisoner bashing is prevalent, as is self-harm or escape attempts to gain attention or to be moved to a different unit or prison. On one occasion, I opened a cell door to see the floor covered in congealed blood; an image that lingers still. The man had been in prison for some twenty years and although he was due to be released, the prisoner had cut his own throat.

As part of the routine, at the end of the day shift all prisoners are locked in for the night and a Duty Officer completes the final lock with the master key, which is then taken to the control room. Once all the cells are double locked, as an officer you have no access to the cell. If you need to get in the cell you have to contact the Duty Officer who would then bring down the key, so it is for emergency use only.

On night duty, I was called to a cell by a prisoner through the intercom system (every cell has an intercom), the cell door is solid steel with a small trapdoor installed. After opening the trapdoor to see and speak to the prisoner, I could see a pool of blood on the floor; he was covered in blood and demanding to go to the infirmary. He had cut his wrists with a razor blade and all I could do was to notify the Duty Officer to bring down the master key, run to the storeroom, grab a towel and hand it to him. It took some twenty minutes before we could get him to the infirmary (every South Australian prison has a manned 24-hour infirmary).

When a person accused of a crime is deemed mentally unfit to stand trial, or a court has found them not guilty by reason of mental illness, they can be sent to James Nash House — a purpose-built prison to house twenty-six inmates, it had solid high walls with revolving drums on top to stop prisoners escaping. Resident inmates are dangerous prisoners who are heavily sedated to control their violent behaviour.

While at Yatala Labour Prison, at times we had to deal with the more severe criminal under normal procedures and an escort officer was needed for such a prisoner whose crime was having brutally murdered his mother — cutting her up, boiling parts of her body and eating them. It was a toss of the coin as to who would be the escorting officer handcuffed and tethered to him, and I lost the toss.

An innocuous item, you might wonder at the harm a shoelace could do — we were called to one of the holding cells by a prisoner to find the prisoner in the cell next to him with a shoelace tied to the bars and around his neck, it does not require a great deal of pressure to affect strangulation.

Camaraderie

Whether you are a Correctional Officer, Police Officer or in the Armed Forces, playing pranks among yourselves is often a vital component of working life — at times relieving the stress and fostering bonds between fellow officers.

I was the target of one such prank. I was always content with being a general Duty Officer as opposed to sitting in an office making decisions in a supervisory role, but there was an unspoken requirement that we all had to at some time 'act up' in this role in light of the possibility of future promotion.

I was not an officer who arrived half an hour early for duty; my timing was always closer to start time, and on this particular weekend, it was my turn to be in charge of the unit. Rushing up the stairwell steps to ensure I was on good time, and so as to set a good example to the other officers, I reached the officer's station door only to find to my fellow officers sitting inside with feet up on the desk, smoking and holding cups of coffee, out of uniform and shirtless.

Chapter 3

TO THE RIOT — MONDAY, MAY 6TH, 1996

I was to find out some years later through the *Freedom of Information* document regarding the riot that certain officers within my unit were deemed to be in danger of loss of life or assault — the reason for my duty change on that day. As previously stated, being a

Correctional Officer is not an easy job, and if you consider the reality that goes hand-in-hand with the job, you are *also* serving time, for as officer and prisoner share the same environment, the inherent close quarters often prove to be a breeding ground for issues and can impact on one's life and wellbeing.

The roster system covered the twenty-four-hour day cycle, but there was respite from routine by means of: night shift (as prisoners are locked down); tower duties; cell searching; gate control duties; hospital watch; visits; court and funeral duties; and prisoner escorts to name a few. Despite ensuring variety in the job design, being a Unit Officer on the other hand was and is a constant commitment. Within the shared experience of the institutional environment, the difference is that at the end of your shift *you* get to go home.

From the time of my assignment as a Correctional Officer in January 1989, I had always been at Yatala Labour Prison, the first three and a half years I was consigned to E Division and then transferred to B Division. Security-based classifications were at the time as follows. E Division — prisoner security classifications for assessment, prisoner induction, and B

Division — high and medium security, and prisoners requiring protection.

Yatala Labour Prison G division, which had been purpose-built to house prisoners who were by nature violent or unpredictable in their behaviour, had an extremely tight security level. Prisoners were allocated single cells and exercised in separate yards, with no contact with other inmates; their movements individually controlled by up to four officers at a time.

B Division, where I was a serving officer at the time of the riot, comprised three floors: a ground floor and two upper floors, with each floor divided into two units — West and East units. The upper floor of B Division was commonly known as 'B Top'. As a general rule, prisoners in this area were serving long sentences and were given a higher security rating than prisoners in other parts of the prison. Once a prisoner demonstrated that they would abide by prison rules and regulations, he would be transferred to F Division, which was the division where prisoners were permitted to work in various industrial occupations.

The ground floor was predominately inmates who were considered non-conformists within the prison system, while Protectees, as the name implies, were housed on the second floor.

B Top's unit divisions — B Top West and B Top East comprised thirty-one individual cells accommodating thirty-one inmates and twenty-nine cells on the East side. To gain access to the East and West units, which were all single and locked from the outside, one had to pass through the main and lockable barrier gate to the unit.

B Top Events

Between each B Top unit there was a small area and a barrier consisting of vertical steel bars situated centrally between each unit. Adjacent to the barriers were solid-steel fire doors, which could slide across, enabling access to the central area from the stairwell or lift. A stairwell led to the central area from the ground floor, and once through the securely locked barrier gate you entered the Western section, which was my rostered position on that day.

Facilitating the operating system, on the right side of the unit there were two cells — a room for cleaning utilities and an officer's station. Visually, the lockable station featured a large glass window that overlooked the open space common area, food servery section, north and south barrier gates and the Manager's Office. Practically, the station was our working office where prisoner unit records were kept in a filing cabinet, housing basic amenities such as telephones, chairs, washbasin, fridge, hot water jug for coffee, and a lockable toilet.

On the left side of the B Top West entrance there was a laundry storeroom (prisoner's clothing, detergents and hygienic liquids such as Hexol and a filing cabinet) and one cell leading into an open area where there was a bench with a food servery section. On either side there was a South and North side wing for prisoner accommodation cells; each wing having fourteen individual cells, a shower area and at the end of each wing an exit fire door. Adjacent to the South wing gate was the Manager's Office.

As I was on Swing Shift, which was a late afternoon shift, I would not have a lunch break which I usually used for training, but I had cycled four kilometres, completed a light gym workout, showered and changed, off to work for an 11.30 am start. Swing Shift was then associated with duties like performing urine analysis tests on inmates, cell searching, relieving duties, escorts and visits, and although not the normal routine unit duties as such, it provided a break from the constant demands of the prisoners.

Normality soon vanished as upon arriving for duty I had my rostered position changed to unit day officer position, which meant I was to be working on the Top floor of B1 West acting as Unit Officer for the shift. My duties entailed the movements of inmates, seeing to any requests they might have and the assessment of new inmates.

Between 11.30 am and 13:00 hours I was stationed in the unit office with Officer Smyth. The prisoners were confined to their cells over lunch. The afternoon routine did not begin until after 13:00 when the prisoners headed off to recreation areas, education rooms or work duties, some remaining in their respective wings. The recreational movement allocation usually went for about two hours, after which prisoners would return to their respective units between 15:00 and 15:20 ready for the nightly lock-down procedure.

This day, approximately ten prisoners had remained in the wings, so we continued with our duties as required, the only exception being the return of prisoner Yuille. After having been assaulted in the recreation yard, he had been struck in the right eye and had some facial bruising. In general, prisoners do not 'give up' on other prisoners and in principle would not tell a Unit Officer anything. The only reason to 'dob in' another prisoner would be for some benefit or gain; even then it would be to a manager or senior officer in exchange for a cell movement, transfer to another prison or a protection unit.

Officer Smyth received instructions to prepared Yuille for a transfer to the lower security F Division, and within a short period of time after Yuille's return, prisoner Dennison, who had remained in the unit, requested to speak to the Unit Manager Mr Holt. As Holt was not present, Dennison was allowed to speak to Unit Supervisor Jones, so he was then escorted from the unit around 13:30, appearing nervous and shaking.

Later in the shift we received information that Dennison was going to sign himself into a protection unit and in light of Yuille's assault, one could only assume that he was going to 'dob in' other prisoners as he was fearing for his own safety, and so it was that at approximately 14:15 prisoner Yuille was transferred to F Division by other officers.

Thinking it time for coffee and a sit down, I waited for the return of prisoners from the recreation areas, education rooms and work duties.

Officer Jones, who was the Acting Assistant Manager on the day, had returned to the Unit Manager's Office, while Officer Smith, who was rostered on a different unit had come into B Top West unit to use the office toilet.

Just after 15:00 the B division front entrance office asked if we were ready to receive prisoners from Recreation Yard 7, to which we responded in the affirmative, Officer Smyth left the office and proceeded to the B1 West unit barrier gate to unlock for prisoner movement into the unit. I then exited the office and stood in the middle of the walkway where I could see Officer Smyth standing about a metre inside the open barrier gate.

It was only a minute or two before the prisoners began entering the unit through the main barrier. They were walking normally towards me as I stood facing them in the middle of the walkway leading to the North and South wings, they would then branch off to their respective wings. Leading the inmates was Van Der Haag and on either side were Preston, Ogden and Tuckwell.

When Van Der Haag got to where I was standing, I moved to my left and turned towards the north wing entrance to unlock the gate and in the same motion was reaching to unhook my keys off my belt on the left side, when suddenly I heard Van Der Haag's voice suddenly yell out, *'Get them!'*

I turned, but this was to no advantage as I was immediately jumped on by a number of prisoners. I was punched around the head as they were trying to force me to the ground. I was still standing, my face covered in blood and my left eye closed, stooped over trying to fend off the continuous barrage of punches.

Endeavouring to head towards the laundry door, I was on the right side of the walkway entrance leading to the main unit barrier gate. Why I chose this direction I don't know, perhaps any direction of escape at the time seemed good.

I was being forced towards the ground, but my determination to stand up was solid after years of playing football and nightclub security. At all cost, I knew I had to try not go to ground because that is where you are the most vulnerable. Fit and strong from many years of sport and hard training, I was beginning to free myself when a prisoner yelled out, 'Grab him 'round the neck — he's breaking clear!'

Immediately a prisoner put a headlock on me and at the same time we hit the filing cabinet next to the laundry door and the impact of hitting it released his grip from around my neck. Looking up I saw the open unit barrier gate to my left — this was my exit and I headed towards it but again I was jumped on and forced onto my hands and knees. By this time, my left eye was bloodied and closed; the kicks and punches just kept coming but the numbness in my body was preventing me from feeling their effect. I started to crawl towards the unit barrier gate with blows raining down on me; then all of a sudden there was this penetrating voice from prisoner Yates who repeatedly yelled, '*Go down, Mr Werchon! Go down, Boss! Go down, Boss!*' Looking back, from his perspective he was saying if you become submissive the prisoners are less likely to continue beating you, but this was something that I was not accustomed to. I had not been in this situation before — escaping was my only objective.

By this time, I was about three metres from the unit barrier and the tension from within my body relaxed for a moment, thinking that by now the prison alarm siren would have gone off alerting officers of a prisoner attack on a fellow officer or officers and a veritable cavalry of officers would come charging through the unit barrier gate.

In front of me was the open gate and freedom — a short distance to safety — one metre to go ...

Standing in front of the open unit barrier gate were four officers; my immediate thoughts were *it's over.*

The officers standing in the doorway froze with panic in their eyes and to my shock and utter disbelief, they shut the unit barrier gate. I do not know how else to describe what was happening before me, as I looked into their eyes the recent echoing voice of prisoner Yates to '*Go down, Mr Werchon!*' was now a reality, in truth there was now no chance of escape. The closing of the gate effectively sealed my fate ...

> Why the officers shut the barrier I can only speculate — only they and their consciences can answer that question. Much later, during one of my recovery visits I mentioned to the psychiatrist how abandoned I had felt. Oddly it reminded me of the final scene in the film *Von Ryan's Express,* where Frank Sinatra is running to catch the train leaving the tunnel; just as he almost reaches the handrail, he trips and is

left to his fate. Having crossed the line between life and death, this proved to be the pivotal point for me, and a defining moment in the events that transpired. What was unfolding before their eyes was real, not a training drill, and while judging another person's actions when you are not in their situation is difficult, they alone bear the brunt.

I presume the obvious answer is containment of the situation, but then two of the officers were specially trained response officers allowing for four officers to be locked in with thirty-two volatile prisoners who were now in control of the west unit. These prisoners were serving time for crimes such as murder, rape, and violent assault. Their respect for authority was low and they were unpredictable in their actions, as power and violence is prevalent within the prisoner structure. Violent, extremely angry, bloodthirsty prisoners on a mad rampage of destruction; we were now in the hands of fate and, more importantly — God's hands.

I stopped crawling and then prisoner Van Der Haag's voice echoed through the commotion, *'If you try and open the gate, I WILL kill him!'*

Another shouted, *'I'll smash him with a fire hydrant!'*

The prisoners then dragged me by my trouser belt away from the unit barrier and for a moment my struggle had ceased. They dragged me back face down on my hands and knees to cell 502, which was the first on the left side of the south wing and unceremoniously threw me head-first into the cell. I landed on Officer Smyth who appeared to be unconscious with his torso propped up on the bed and the lower part of his body on the floor and his back against the bed, arms outstretched, blood over his face.

He began to regurgitate, so I immediately lifted myself off him and sat on the edge of bed. (The prison cells are approximately four by two metres with a bed, small table, chair, toilet and wash basin). As I looked towards the open cell door, a prisoner wearing a homemade balaclava came through the doorway and with both hands began wielding a white iron bar that he had held over his right shoulder — a table leg that had been broken from a tabletop. As he swung the bar towards Officer Smyth, I reacted by moving up towards the prisoner using my left arm as a shield; the impact of the bar on my left forearm caused such considerable pain; I thought my arm was broken. The next blow hit my right cheekbone and continued down onto my right shoulder. My left arm was hanging, and I could not lift my right arm, so I had to wear a further blow to my right shoulder again. My strength was ebbing away and as he raised the bar again, I knew very soon that I would be unable to fend off the blows.

As if a bolt of lightning had struck him, prisoner Yates burst through the doorway edging his way between the prisoner and myself saying menacingly, 'We are not going this far.' At that, the prisoner with the iron bar left the cell and Officer Jones was dragged into the cell face up and backwards and unceremoniously thrown on top of Officer Smyth. Officer Jones was conscious and rolled off Officer Smyth, ending up slumped against the side wall at the end of the bed. His face was completely bloodied, which was a disturbing sight, and I began to wonder how far the prisoners were prepared to go. Prickles of fear crept into my body, but I also knew from training one has to try not to show fear while at the same time not spitting in their face. Self-control and the power to reason with the prisoners had to prevail.

My father, who had been in the Victorian Police Force, had once given me advice on how to handle aggressive situations — always keep calm and not be too submissive or too provocative if caught in such a situation — this advice certainly helped me throughout the riot, focusing on survival and thinking of once again being with my loved ones.

Officer Jones had only recently returned back to work after some considerable time off due to a heart condition, and he lay in the corner of the cell saying, 'I think I am going to have a heart attack.' This allowed me to speak to prisoner Yates, who along with Gibson, stood in the entrance of the doorway, which to my thinking seemed like he was acting as a guard. I thought then that there was light at the end of the tunnel. I urged Gibson that we *had* to get Officer Smyth who was still unconscious, and Officer Jones who could be having a heart attack, out for urgent medical attention, adding that Officer Smyth could die as he was struggling to breathe. I had no sooner spoken when Officer Smith was brought into the cell bleeding profusely from his head and left ear. Prisoner Gibson and another prisoner entered the cell carrying First Aid kits followed by prisoner Stephens who I spoke to, reiterating the seriousness of officers Jones and Smyth's conditions, and if I could use a radio to ask for medical help and their release. By this time, prisoner Gibson had managed to get Officer Smyth onto the bed and was rendering first aid by clearing his throat of vomit so that he could breathe. Prisoner Stephens allowed me to make a radio call to the control room using Officer Jones' radio that was still attached to his belt.

> Later, during the court trial, I made mention of prisoner Yates' courage throughout the riot, his role being one of protector, giving aid where it was needed. In doing so he placed himself at significant risk from other prisoners. Prisoner Yates stated that he was approached by other prisoners before the riot but told them he wanted no part of it, despite threats toward him. He had no choice but to return to the unit when the time came for the movement of all prisoners and on arriving in B Top West Division, the riot commenced. Due to his actions, he later was given a shot at freedom and said on his release, 'There is not a chance I will blow it.' He then broke down and hugged his mother and girlfriend in court. He was released on a suspended sentence and placed on a two-year good behaviour bond more than a year after being charged over the riot at Yatala Labour Prison.

Yatala prison, originally called The Stockade, was named after the Hundred of Yatala (roughly the historic District council of Yatala) ...

... The word 'Yatala' is from the Weira group of the Kaurna Aboriginal people, meaning 'water running by the side of a river'. It is known as a Labour prison by virtue of its vast industries complex and the use of convict labour in its construction ...

... Today, the prison holds high-, medium- and low-security prisoners, and is South Australia's main

induction and reception prison for male prisoners. It still retains industry facilities that are the largest in the South Australian prison system and is run by the South Australian Government's Department for Correctional Services. Some of the original buildings and parts of old equipment can still be seen from a creek-level walking trail, between the prison and new suburb of Walkley Heights. These include guard towers, quarries, a blacksmith's shop and a gunpowder magazine ...

The prison has been expanded many times but still has functioning buildings that date to the 1850s. It remains Adelaide's main male prison ...

'We're not going to take that bulls..t off them any more.

Enough's enough. We want what we want and we are going to get it.'

Protest sign on the top level of B Division says:

'you're asking for it'

15:35 The call for medical assistance

After identifying myself to the control room and my request for urgent medical help, prisoner Stephens snatched the radio from me and that was the last time I saw it.

Prisoners Yates and Gibson then began rendering first aid to myself and Officers Jones, Smyth and Smith. Prisoner Gibson wrapped a white bandage around my bloodied and closed left eye. Prisoner Stephens then returned to the cell, stating that the prisoners had agreed to the release of officers Jones and Smyth, and then promptly left. This immediate promise was short lived though, as I could hear him arguing with prisoner Van Der Haag in the walkway. Van Der Haag firmly stating, 'No, we don't release any.'

Stephens replied, 'Well they are serious.'

Another prisoner decided, 'Well, we'll let one go — whoever is the most serious.'

Throughout all of this I could hear the uproar of prisoners smashing furniture and equipment outside of the cell. Mattresses were being dragged past the cell towards the end of the wing, which clearly would be used to barricade the south wing emergency exit. The noise was amplified by the walls.

The yelling and shouting was continuous — '*Kill 'em!*', '*We mean it this time!*' This was a full-scale riot. '*We tried to negotiate peacefully.*', '*This time we will give them some dead bodies.*'

Being in a confined space with nowhere to go and hearing all the commotion going on outside was daunting and frightening as at the time I could only think how their words might come true. Prisoner Yates was heard to say, 'Just stay here and don't come out.' And later, 'Just *shut up*.'

Who in his right mind would venture outside the cell? Hearing what was going on was beyond words — how do you evaluate fear and the uncertainty of the prisoners' behaviour? This irrational terror was being directed at us and our system of authority; myself and the other officers had nowhere to run or hide, trapped with thirty-two inmates in a brick cage with our loved ones on the outside praying for our quick and safe release. *Be calm*, show no fear, *work with the prisoner* I repeated in my head, *and you might walk away from this nightmare*.

Then a group of prisoners came into the cell grabbing Officer Jones by the ankles and dragging him out;

this was the last I was to see of him until a few days later at the Adelaide Hospital.

Prisoner Van Der Haag's voice again yelled out in a menacing way, *'Get the other one.'* The prisoners returned again within a short time saying, 'We want one of them out here.'. They grabbed hold of Officer Smith and walked him out of the cell. I did not see him again until just before our release the next morning Tuesday at 02:23.

Prisoner Van Der Haag ordered, 'Get the other one out into the circle.' Immediately prisoners Richards and Preston entered the cell and with one on either side they dragged me into the circle at the centre of the two wings and sat me down on a plastic chair. Bleeding from the face, I had offered no resistance as my body was hurting from head to toe and my energy was depleted from lack of fluids — I was to find out later I had much physical damage from the beating I had incurred.

Surrounded by prisoners, negotiations were proceeding for the release of Officer Jones, and I could see prisoners Stephens and Van Der Haag at the main barrier talking to officers on the other side. There are always defining moments in life that one does not forget, and this was one of them.

As I sat in the chair watching the proceedings, prisoner Prichard, who was standing in front of me, repeatedly waved a long screwdriver back and forth just centimetres from my face in a threatening manner. As this was during the final stage of Officer Jones' release (whom I could not see), the prisoners were tense and obviously very wary of what might occur when the barrier gate was to be opened for his release.

I did not have to wait long for the prisoners' reactions, as the roar of prisoners Van Der Haag's and Stephens' voices echoed down the walkway. '*Shive 'em if they rush in.*' which was warning to all that if the police officers were to rush into the unit, the prisoners guarding myself and officers Smith and Smyth would knife us with any weapon they had at hand. At the time of Jones' release, I didn't know where officers Smyth and Smith were, and I presumed that Officer Smyth was still unconscious in cell 502 where I had last seen him.

I was instructed by the prisoners near me to keep my head down, which I did, and this would have been at the time of Officer Jones' release.

15:39 Lift returned to bottom floor containing medical staff and Officer Jones

I was taken back to cell 502 by prisoners Prichard and Richards, where Officer Smyth still lay on the bed unconscious, all I could do was to sit on the edge of the bed alongside an unconscious man awaiting our fate. Shortly after my return to the cell, prisoner Preston entered armed with a screwdriver and instructed other inmates to take me across the wing to his cell and make me more comfortable. I recall wondering, was this a concern for my wellbeing or was the divide among the prisoners starting to occur? Prisoner Yates stood guard at the entrance of the cell.

> These frightening moments have haunted me to this day as I have always been a person who wants to be in control of events that are happening around me, especially the physical control of my actions. Since the events of the riot that day, I have never had a peaceful night's sleep; constantly waking up and fighting with my thoughts. Fractured nightmares plague me where I am trying to break free of a building, fighting with other people or a force

being applied that restricts my movements. During these nightmares, I have physically smashed in doors, kicked and broken a window (this happened in Finland, and I awoke to snow falling on the bedding through the broken window, just missing my wife), also I have hit out at her during my sleep. I came to very sudden and clear awareness one night when I awoke face down, bleeding from the face after leading an assault attack where we jumped over a wall. To my wife's shock, one night she was awakened by me wrestling with Mighty Mouse in my dreams ...

I have attended all the prescribed programs, treatments and taken medication provided by doctors, physiotherapists, physiologists, psychiatrists, rehabilitation counsellors. I also spent a weekend at hospital when there was a fear that I might self-harm. All of this treatment has had its benefits, but one can become too dependent on this and lose the ability for self-guidance. As another person cannot stand in your shoes for you, eventually, you have to walk in your own. I take no medication now and have not seen a medical consultant for Post-Traumatic Stress Disorder for several years. I am walking in my own shoes, but still need the occasional visit to a physiotherapist.

Outside of Preston's cell the continuous deafening yelling and smashing of equipment was raging. '*Kill them, no hold it*. They're coming up — *get ready*!' Van Der Haag yelled out, '*Is there a killer on each of 'em*?', indicating to me that there were negotiations going on while we awaited our fate. With the destructive noise outside the cell, after about twenty minutes — though it seemed like forever — prisoners Preston and Richards came into the cell, took hold of me and walked me out of the cell into the circle area and sat me down onto a plastic chair for the second time. Prisoner Prichard then tied my ankles and legs with tape to the chair legs, my hands were then placed together in front of me and also bound with tape. To make me feel more uncertain of my fate, prisoner Preston, armed with a green-handled screwdriver, again moved towards me, suggesting to a group of prisoners seated at a table opposite me, 'Let me take out his good eye with the screwdriver.'.

I was petrified as he moved towards me holding the screwdriver at waist height, stopping just in front of me and bringing the tip of the screwdriver within a centimetre of my right eye. *Was I going to lose my eye?* I wondered fearfully. His mood was dangerous and threatening. I was defenceless as my legs and hands were bound tightly; there was little I could do but pray and hope he was not going to take out my eye. Not knowing as to whether I had any vision in my left eye which was now closed and bloodied and covered with a white bandage, added a further concern for my safety.

To my blessed relief, Preston stopped smiling at me and walked away. Immediately, a white pillowcase was pulled over my head and shoulders and there I sat in this position for some three to four hours with the voices of the inmates threatening my wellbeing. Every now and then a prisoner would walk past and slap me around the head. It felt as though it was like Russian roulette — I didn't know which blow would bring a worse fate. After a while each slap did not have as great an impact on me, as my body was already aching all over.

Prisoner Richards sneered for effect. 'We'll cut off his right ear to show we mean business.'

'No, I think we'll start with his index finger and throw that out.' Preston replied.

The intimidation game was now in play with another joining in. 'No, throw some Hexol over him and set him alight.' Their laughter followed, echoing in my head and then I heard and felt the distinct sound and subsequent wet feeling and smell of being urinated on, which was to occur on a number of occasions. Urinating on me was a tactic designed to demonstrate their power. Van Der Haag was unrelenting in his demands that a killer was to be behind me at all times. As an asthma suffer, the pillowcase over my head frightened me and I was having difficulty breathing. To my relief, prisoner Murray became aware of my distress and asked if I was struggling to breathe, to which I replied yes and that I was an asthmatic. Murray then cut a slit in the pillowcase near my mouth and placed a Ventolin puffer to my mouth so that I could get some relief. As my hands were still bound and my fingers were going numb, I asked if he could release some of the tension from my legs and wrists, and he cut the tape from around my legs and removed a little of the tape from around my wrists to loosen my wrists while they still remained bound.

Throughout this ordeal I was occasionally dragged on the chair around and around not knowing where I was going but at times, though, I thought I was near the main unit barrier gate. I also could hear the four ringleaders planning how they would react if the police decided to storm the unit, such things as 'Make sure all the windows are covered.' as they were fearful of the police snipers and frequently reminded each other to keep their heads down. Preston was giving instructions to move me back into a cell, the pillowcase was then removed from my head and as this was happening prisoner Van Der Haag yelled at me not to look up and keep my head down, but out of the corner of my eye I glimpsed four of the ringleaders — prisoners Van Der Haag, Ogden, Stephens, Tuckwell and Morse seated at a table between the two wings, smoking and talking among themselves.

I was taken back to prisoner Preston's cell and here I sat on the bed awaiting the next ordeal and after a little while I heard further commotion from outside the cell.

Prisoner Van Der Haag yelled. *'Get Smyth up to the fire escape door!'* which was at the far end of the south wing. Looking out to the cell opposite me, I could see Officer Smyth laying on the bed still unconscious in cell 502, with prisoner Gibson sitting on the edge of the bed attending to him.

Prisoner Stephens then came into the wing and said, 'We're taking Smyth up to the fire escape door.' Inmates Gibson and Rasmussen then took hold of the bed mattress with Officer Smyth lying on his back unconscious and dragged him towards the southern end of the south wing. Prisoner Stephens entered the cell I was in and used the cell intercom, which was connected to the main control room, to negotiate the release of Officer Smyth. He spoke to a negotiator — Eddie — demanding that the Police Respond Squad move out of the building and onto the grass area so that they could see them, and he also wanted Correctional Officer McKinley to come up the southern wing fire stairwell and unlock the fire door for the release of Officer Smyth.

Sitting on the edge of the cell bed with prisoners Baynes and Richards, who had re-taped my legs together, Prisoner Baynes suddenly started screaming at me to lie face down and not look up. There I was, legs and hands tightly taped together, lying face down, my head at the bedhead near the wall and my feet facing the open door, and I remained in this position while the release of Officer Smyth was proceeding.

There was one prisoner standing at my head end holding a white iron bar and another prisoner near my back holding a screwdriver and they were being instructed by Van Der Haag who stood at the cell door entrance to shiv me if the cops entered the wing during the release of Officer Smyth, I was now anxiously awaiting his release. Prisoner Van Der Haag referred to them as 'killers' and with my strength rapidly being depleted and being hogged-tied, my survival instincts were telling me if I were to hear a bang it could be a gun shot or a Stun Grenade and *just roll off the bed and pray.* I was now in survival mode, and my mind was a confused mess. I thought of my family — Liisa and my beautiful girls — and I prayed to have the opportunity to hug them again.

> I was told later by the police that they had considered entering the unit by force and, that at the time, as the only other officer in the unit was Officer Smith, they would have had a limited timeframe to get to both he and myself. This action was aborted, so in hindsight, rolling onto the floor may have worked.

Over the intercom I could hear that the prisoners had managed to get Officer Smyth out onto the stairwell landing, but they were having trouble shutting the fire door. This was causing some panic among the prisoners as they were fearful of the Police Response Squad using this opportunity to enter the wing. After a while, the fire door was shut but had not been locked because the control room had to activate the electronics of the fire door for it to be secured.

Once the fire door was secured, the tension among the prisoners started to ease as the immediate danger to them had passed. Not so for me though, I was still their hostage, and they were unsure of what was going on outside the unit.

21:34 Officer Smyth exited fire exit via door 47, placed on a stretcher, assisted by Mr McKinley and Detective Lewis.

Prisoner Baynes then entered the cell and I was allowed to turn over and sit on the edge of the bed. He then untied my hands and feet, which was a great relief, and I was getting the feeling that the tension within the unit was starting to ease.

The police negotiators were requesting our release and the prisoners were demanding a statement on television. Prisoner Stephens again entered the cell and said to me, 'You will be out in fifteen minutes, Boss, after CEO Vidler reads a statement on television.' This did not happen though and over the next three hours he entered the cell on occasion and spoke to the control room about the proceedings, which seemed to have come to a halt.

During this time, various other prisoners came into the cell to talk and make me coffee. I also had a cigarette, which was something out of the ballpark for me as I do not smoke and never have. The atmosphere had relaxed somewhat, and I surmised that more than likely the possible consequences of their actions was beginning to play on their consciences. I considered what might happen to them if the Police Response Squad did crash through the barriers and doors. Of the thirty-two inmates, only eight or nine were ringleaders and the rest had been caught up in the action and would be obliged to participate for their own safety. Now that the initial violence and destruction had passed, their own safety would be uppermost in their minds and the division among the prisoners was starting to manifest itself.

Prisoner Murray assisted me by strapping my chest

as I was having trouble breathing again and as every movement caused pain, the strapping was of some relief. To this day though, I have always been puzzled by the actions of prisoner Baynes who came into the cell, sat on the table and talked in general about how was I feeling and that it should be over soon. His conversation wasn't directly regarding what was taking place, more so, he kept it light, preferring to ask if he could make me a coffee. At the time of prisoner Baynes entering the cell he was carrying an 18-inch yellow screwdriver, which to my surprise he left on the tabletop when he left to make me a cup of coffee. Thinking back, I did not consider the screwdriver any further and when he returned with the coffee, he picked it up and left. Time was slow and seemed to me never-ending; now we were into early hours of Tuesday morning.

After a while, prisoners Baynes and Yates came into the cell, took hold of me and walked me out of the cell to the unit barrier gate. On the other side of the gate, I could see a number of police negotiators who asked how I was feeling. What do you say with your captives holding you and a locked metal barrier between you and rescue — 'Okay'?

Prisoners Van Der Haag, Stephens and Preston were

also by the gate talking to the police negotiators. I was then taken back to the cell being supported by prisoners Baynes and Yates as it was now some nine hours since the initial attack and my body was aching. I was extremely tired, and my strength was ebbing away slowly but surely. Back in the cell I sat on the bed awaiting the next move the inmates would make and it was not long before I heard prisoner Van Der Haag scream out, '*Move him to the wing!*'. Prisoners Baynes and Yates came into the cell and walked me to the opposite wing — north wing — and sat me on a chair opposite Officer Smith who was sitting on a mattress in the middle of the wing. He had blood on his face and right hand; this was the first time I had seen him since he was taken out of cell 502 just after the initial attack by the prisoners. The prisoners told us not to talk to one another. Then again, we were moved from where we sat to a cell on the western side of the north wing. We were guarded by the prisoners — Preston who was holding a green-handled screwdriver, and Richards who carried a brown straight-edged blade knife, Baynes brandished a metre-long round white iron bar (a broken-off table leg), and Ogden had no weapon.

We sat on the edge of the bed, waiting, not knowing

what was about to happen next, and my mind captured details like the screwdriver and the knife, to this day they remain embedded in my mind.

After a while, prisoners Preston and Baynes left the cell but returned soon after and again, we were escorted out into the north wing and made to sit on chairs in the middle of the wing where we remained closely guarded by prisoners Preston, Richards, Baynes, and Ogden.

Prisoner Baynes mentioned to myself and Officer Smith that negotiations had been made for the prisoners to exit the unit in groups of eight prisoners at a time, so now it was just a final waiting game.

After what seem an eternity, prisoner Baynes said, 'Yous'll be out soon.' and then he and prisoners Richards, Preston, and Ogden walked away towards the unit wing circle, leaving Officer Smith and me alone.

Time seemed to be at a standstill as we waited for the slow process of the prisoners handing themselves over to the police in groups of eight at a time. To my surprise and I suppose disbelief, prisoner Van Der Haag showed a moment of compassion for myself and Officer Smith, or perhaps it was for his own safety.

Suddenly, we heard a very loud commotion coming from the centre circle between the south and north wings, and I then heard prisoner Morse yell out, *'I don't care—I'm going to take one out anyway!'*

Looking towards the circle, I saw inmate Morse heading our way, armed with his makeshift iron bar that he was holding in both hands. *This is it,* I thought, his final act of vengeance in the dying minutes of this nightmare. His hatred and anger towards the system was so deep that he had to go out with one final attempt to harm us — those who represented the system.

Just before he reached us, from out of nowhere Van Der Haag appeared, who moved quickly towards Morse and pushed him up against the wing wall. 'If you're going to do that, we're gonna have it cut *now*.' With that Morse stopped and they both then walked back to the wing circle.

When all the other prisoners had left the unit, prisoners Van Der Haag and Stephens came back down the wing; Van Der Haag assisted me, and Stephens assisted Smith. We all did the final walk to the B Top West unit barrier gate of the top floor — for maybe the last time.

Van Der Haag used me as a shield as we left B Top,

and prisoner Stephens used Officer Smith as a shield. I feel that perhaps this was to protect themselves from harm, given the deep distrust for us as Correctional Officers and thus, part of the system. Alternatively, it may have been that bravado was not in their make-up.

02:23 Tuesday Officers Werchon and Smith exit B Top West, assisted down centre stairwell, treated at the scene and conveyed to hospital by ambulance.

The police wasted no time in getting my statement and as I was cohesive and not concussed, Police Officer Snell and fellow Correctional Officer Collins rode with me in the ambulance taking the early parts of my statement as we travelled. I was tired, bruised and battered from the bashings and loss of blood; when I arrived at the Royal Adelaide Hospital, I was rushed to the emergency room where a team of doctors and nurses addressed my wounds. And with medication, finally sleep, a very deep sleep, which was a great relief.

Liisa, who had been waiting all night in the reception room for my release, had the opportunity to whisper in my ear that she loved me as I was being wheeled to the ambulance with my eyes covered and a neck brace on. She'd had to drive herself to the hospital where she was able to see and talk to me.

During the week I was in hospital there was a constant barrage of officers and government officials including the Premier of the day to wish me a speedy recovery, plus the usual get-well cards, flowers and occasional chocolate.

Liisa and the girls came in to visit me every day. I clearly remember my youngest daughter, who was six at the time, had come to the hospital to visit me for the first time and as she was walking towards the room I was in, I was being wheeled down the same hallway from the opposite direction in a wheelchair after an X-ray. As we reached each other I spoke to her, Mikaela did not recognise me. Even though Liisa said, 'That is Dad.' I was unrecognisable to her with my swollen head and bloodied eyes, and she ran to hide behind Liisa.

As a result of the beatings my immediate injury symptoms were constant headaches due to head injuries; cervical, thoracic and lumbar spinal pain; left shoulder pain; left elbow numbness; chest wall pain; right ankle pain and the mental scars of anxiety, depression, agitation, PTSD and sleep disturbance.

When I was first examined on 11 May 1996 by my personal physician, the report was as follows:

> ... The injuries were bruising, haematoma and swelling of both eyes, a left subconjunctival haemorrhage, a two-centimetre laceration of the left upper eyebrow, bruising of the right lower chest, the left chest and the posterior left shoulder. There was also bruising of the right upper chest, right deltoid area, the left upper arm and swelling of the left elbow. There were abrasions of both knees from when Mr Werchon was dragged along the floor and the chest bruising was from kicking injuries. Mr Werchon had been struck by an iron bar on the right cheekbone, the back of his right shoulder and the left elbow. There were also multiple small abrasions and lacerations of the scalp from boot injuries. In my opinion, Mr Werchon will never be fit to resume pre-accident employment. Mr Werchon will not be fit in the future for employment where he is subject to psychological stress or any stress to the injuries which have resulted in permanent disability. Mr

> Werchon's disabilities and resultant loss of work capacity would make it extremely difficult if not impossible for any suitable future employment to be found ...

There is often a downside to unfortunate events that will have a bearing on you for the rest of your life.

The report clearly was not favourable, and it was not until the year 1997 that my body would begin to respond to the constant physiotherapy treatments and medication, which permitted me to walk with ease. At first, I experienced weight gain from lack of exercise and the effects of medication. Later, light jogging assisted and the associated flexibility that eventually came lent strength to again lift weights and resume full-body exercises. The self-confidence was to take a few more years through the help and guidance of psychotherapy treatment and still to present day, I've seldom had a good night's sleep. The injuries to my body resurface from time to time, which affects my flexibility and strength, but I continue to keep exercising and this is to my benefit, while an irregular heart rhythm beat, which was a result of the incident, is now a constant part of my life.

Chapter 4

TRIAL

The committal trial commenced at the Sir Samuel Way Building in Victoria Square on 26 November 1996 under intense security. Presiding over the hearing and the seven accused prisoner ringleaders was Magistrate D.

During the committal hearing Justice D was obliged to warn the accused that if they did not stop laughing and chatting among themselves, he would remand them straight to trial. The prisoners faced a total of eighteen charges relating to the four prison officers who were bashed, urinated on and kept prisoner on the night of 6 May and the following day 7 May during a riot in B Wing at the Yatala Labour Prison. They were also charged with assaulting other officers during the riot. No laughing matter.

During the opening submission, the Crown Prosecutor told the court the riot was designed to '*maximise injury, property damage and disruption*'. She further stated that the prisoners were being escorted back into the wing about 3.15 pm after their daily exercise, when prison officers Werchon and Smyth were jumped by the prisoners. Continuing:

> ... one prisoner yelled '*Get them*', just prior to the attack. ... sitting in an office, was attacked with an iron bar and stabbed in the arm while ... heard a commotion while in the toilet and walked out to see another officer being bashed. ... tried to assist but was forced back into the toilets before being smoked out by a fire lit at the door. The prisoners then allegedly ransacked the wing on the orders of ...

The first of two days in court — 27 November 1996 — was like reliving the whole event over again and again, as the seven accused prisoners and their defence lawyers were right there. By days' end I was a nervous wreck after being constantly questioned by each individual lawyer repeatedly. I was secured in a room speaking via a closed-circuit television to the court room and while I had a limited view of the court, all in the court had a full view of me.

Then to top it off, I was questioned as to certain documents that I had in my possession and to how I had come to have them with me. The file of notes I had with me were taken from me on arrival. I presumed they'd been scrutinised by the Court duty officer before being brought back into the room. Not once did I open or look at them during the hearing. When asked to identify the documents' source, I declined on the grounds that it could incriminate me. The hearing was adjourned, and my lawyer and I were ushered into the chambers. Under pain of imprisonment, I was given the directive to name the source, to which I again declined. Needless to say, I had a very restless night and many anxious days awaiting my next court hearing.

As if Lady Luck was shining on me during the next appearance, after the third refusal to divulge the source, they revealed themselves in the courtroom and explained to court their reasons for passing on the information.

On 30 November 1996, the seven accused prisoners of the Yatala Labour Riot were committed to stand trial.

At the trial, held on 23 September 1997 the prisoners finally pleaded guilty and had their sentence times increased.

As a final note, it is my opinion that the justice system is questionable or at the very least flawed, given that the longest extension applied was three years and six months, moreover, some of these prisoners were already serving life imprisonment.

It begs the question — what *is* and *is not* one's total life?

* * *

Epilogue

Never one to give in, I was persistent in my desire to get back into the workforce. By the end of the year 1996 I was starting to gain self-confidence and experienced a strong desire to move on and stop being a pawn in the Work Cover system. My body was healing, light running was possible, and my strength levels were also high by this time. Reality was setting in, and it was slowly dawning on me that the prospects of returning to the prison system as a Correctional Officer was becoming somewhat out of my reach, so I started to pursue the option of a different career path. With the help of my local MP, we were able to get the

Department of Correctional Services to allow me to go to TAFE as a full-time student to study a course in the Advanced Certificate in Physical Recreation (Fitness). For me this was a bonus as I had always been involved in sport and fitness and had previously in 1985 obtained a Health and Fitness Centres Instructors Certificate of Accreditation, which was sponsored by Keiran O'Neil who had a large fitness centre where I was a casual fitness instructor.

My other employment at this time was a door host at exclusive night clubs, which had been my initial leaning towards the career path as a Correctional Officer. While studying at TAFE, I was able to obtain a hands-on training role in the gym at the South Australian Institute of Sport for four hours a week as part of my course assignment. At year's end 1997, I had successfully completed the course, but there were no immediate openings within the government departments, so early in 1998 I accepted a supernumerary position at the Department of Correctional Services' head office, in a clerical role where I remained for a short period of time. However, filing documents and shuffling papers was too inactive and I suppose it was fortunate for me and my sanity that the position was only short term, so it was back to the Work Cover merry-go-round.

With luck, though, I saw a position as an Australian Protective Services Officer and as I again was feeling self-confident and fit in body, I applied. By then I had returned to a high level of fitness and had little trouble in passing their fitness level requirements. Successful at the interview, I was selected to commence a 5-week training course at the South Australian Police Academy starting Monday 31 August 1998.

All went well until Graduation Day in the last week of the course. I was assigned as a Protective Services Officer with duties at Woomera in the Mid North of South Australia. But upon a thorough check of my medical history, they could not offer me a position as an APS Officer. I hadn't mentioned the hostage incident at Yatala, or that I had been diagnosed as having incurred PTSD, and it had come back to haunt me.

> ... On the basis of the information provided and my examination of Mr Werchon, I am unable to recommend his appointment as a Protective Services Officer on medical grounds. I consider that the nature of the duties of a Protective Services Officer,

> and the associated training, pose an unacceptable risk of exacerbating his condition and compromising the efficient and safe performance of the duties required ...

At least they did initially inform me face-to-face and not by letter or phone, as is sometimes the case. Although a blow, this wasn't the end of the world, as while in training at the South Australian Police Academy I came into contact with a fellow Correctional Officer who had been redeployed to the Academy as a Self Defence Trainer and because of the high number of police cadets, there was a position available as a Fitness Coordinator and Trainer. Thus, it proved to be to my advantage as I had attained the Advanced Certificate in Physical Recreation (Fitness) at the TAFE College in 1997.

Along with my knowledge and experience as a sportsman and previous experience managing fitness centres, I had a little help again from my local MP, who had instigated my enrolment in 1997 at the TAFE College. Then followed a meeting he had arranged for Liisa and I with the Deputy Premier of Parliament, so that I could put forward my case for not wanting to stay on Work Cover.

I was back into full-time employment 1999 at the South Australian Police Academy as a Fitness Coordinator and Trainer in a role that I had enthusiasm and a passion for. I was to remain in this position until the middle of 2003, and then with the family made a lifestyle change to move to Cairns where I reside to this present day.

John Werchon — 2000 Sonkjarvi Finland.
Annual wife-carrying competition — not my wife ...